The Living Way

The Living Way

THE
LIVING WAY

By Lillian De Waters

AUTHOR OF

THINKING HEAVENWARD
JOURNEYING ONWARD
WITHIN THE VEIL
GLAD TIDINGS

DAVIS & BOND
PUBLISHERS . BOSTON

Copyright 1912
Lillian DeWaters

LINCOLN & SMITH PRESS . BOSTON

"*I am the way, the truth, the life,*"
  Our blessed Master said;
And whoso to the Father comes
  Must in my pathway tread.

A way, it is not hedged with forms,
  A truth, too large for creeds,
A life, indwelling, deep, and broad,
  That meets the heart's great needs.

To point that living *way; to speak*
  That truth "which makes men free,"
To bring that quick'ning life from heav'n,
  Is highest ministry.

Anon.

He that dwelleth in the secret place of the Most High shall abide under the shadow of the Almighty.

I will say of the Lord, he is my refuge and my fortress: my God; in him will I trust.

Surely he shall deliver thee from the snare of the fowler, and from the noisome pestilence.

He shall cover thee with his feathers, and under his wings shalt thou trust: his truth shall be thy shield and buckler.

Thou shalt not be afraid for the terror by night; nor for the arrow that flieth by day;

Nor for the pestilence that walketh in darkness; nor for the destruction that wasteth at noonday.

A thousand shall fall at thy side, and ten thousand at thy right hand; but it shall not come nigh thee.

Only with thine eyes shalt thou behold and see the reward of the wicked.

Because thou hast made the Lord, which is my refuge, even the Most High, thy habitation;

There shall no evil befall thee, neither shall any plague come nigh thy dwelling.

For he shall give his angels charge over thee, to keep thee in all thy ways.

They shall bear thee up in their hands, lest thou dash thy foot against a stone.

Thou shalt tread upon the lion and adder: the young lion and the dragon shalt thou trample under feet.

Because he has set his love upon me, therefore will I deliver him: I will set him on high, because he hath known my name.

He shall call upon me, and I will answer him: I will be with him in trouble; I will deliver him, and honor him.

With long life will I satisfy him, and show him my salvation.

Psalm 91.

The Living Way

He that dwelleth in the secret place of the Most High shall abide under the shadow of the Almighty.

He that continueth in that spiritual consciousness which is a secret unknown to the worldly-minded and is apart from all wrong thinking shall stand firm under the protection of divine Love.

Mortals are fast finding out that thinking rightly will transform them. Faces and lives can be transformed by true thinking.

Since the stream of thought is constantly flowing, it is inevitable that we shall think something every instant. How necessary it is, then, that we form a right basis for our thoughts! If we think as God thinks, we are thinking rightly.

Unless one discovers the spiritual value of the Bible, his study will fall short of disclosing to him its real importance. The gospel needs only to be understood in its original simplicity to prove itself the means of salvation to every one who applies its teachings.

Right thinking and right living are at hand. Right thoughts will give birth to right actions, to right speech, and to right conditions. Before we can dwell or continue "in the secret place," we must learn how to think rightly about all things; for in this way only shall we receive the protection so lovingly promised.

To know God aright is life eternal, and is our only safeguard. Therefore, before we can dwell "in the secret place" or attain a consciousness sufficiently spiritual to protect us from evil conditions, we must have a correct understanding of God.

Come, then, "and let us reason together" on this all-important subject,— God.

The Scriptures tell us that God is Love. God is the Life of all being. He is Spirit, Soul, Mind. If He is of purer eyes than to behold evil and is altogether lovely, He necessarily sees and knows no evil. It is plain that infinite Good can know nothing of evil, that infinite or all-filling Life can know nothing of death, and that infinite Truth can know nothing but that which originates within itself.

If God is infinite, He fills all reality, and there is nothing except it is in God, for infinity has no limitations. Do we not read in the Bible, "If I make my bed in hell, behold, thou art there"? There is no absence of God. Even if our thoughts dwell in utter darkness or discord, still God is really present.

If God is Love, He is ever-loving and has no consciousness of wrath.

If God is omnipresent, then God's love and power are actively with us.

If God is omniscient, then He is all knowledge, and there is nothing true except that which originates in Him.

If God is omnipotent, He is not merely the strongest power, but He is the *only* power, and hence there can be no power in the universe but God.

Can evil dwell in good? or hate abide in love? Is there any possibility for darkness where light is? The answer must always be in the negative. Then evil conditions have no God-given or legitimate cause, no creator, no right to exist. Love will put hate to flight, understanding will utterly obliterate ignorance, truth will overcome every lie. So God, the Light of the world, the centre and circumference of being, can utterly wipe out every sin, sickness, and discord in our thoughts and in our lives. It only remains for us to know God aright, for it is this truth that will make us free.

In proportion as we become acquainted with God do we become spiritually-minded and dwell "in the secret place of the Most High" and stand under the protection of divine Love. We need have no fear of calamities if we are thinking, living, and demonstrating God's love and truth in our daily lives.

But where shall wisdom be found? and where is the place of understanding? Acquaint now thyself with God, and be at peace.—Job.

THE LIVING WAY

I will say of the Lord, he is my refuge and my fortress: my God; in him will I trust.

I will declare that God is my shelter and my security. Upon Him alone will I rely.

Are we trusting the divine Source alone for our joys, our health, our prosperity? It is wise to ask, How much of my trust am I placing in God?

If we are looking to any other power besides God as able to increase our joys, preserve our health, and widen our means of usefulness, we are breaking the first and greatest commandment,—"Thou shalt have no other gods before me."

The Bible is the revelation of Truth, Life, and Love to humanity. The help which it has for man is a present help. Did not the Psalmist sing, "God is a very present help in time of trouble?"

To the mourner, the despondent, the sick, and the sinner divine Love says: "Come unto me, and I will give you rest." Come into the perfect understanding of God, and you will rest from your sorrows, your sicknesses and sins; and as you clothe yourself in righteousness,—right thinking, will you manifest joy, health, and holiness.

When we are disturbed in thought or in body, do we look to God, the Source of our being, our very life itself, for restoration? or do we rush for a pill or plaster, and look to man and matter for mental and bodily harmony?

Listen to the voice of Spirit: "Bless the Lord, . . . who healeth all thy diseases."

The matter of sickness and suffering has so large a bearing upon our happiness as to merit our serious consideration. The relation between health and religion is becoming more and more apparent each day. Why should not a Christian take God literally for what He is, and accept nothing else?

Why is it that a prayer to God, the Creator of the universe and man, the Father whose son is the Saviour of the world, is generally believed to have less healing virtue than a pill or a spoonful of medicine? It is a lack of understanding or of confidence in God which causes man to rely upon other than spiritual means in time of trouble.

Consider the lilies how they grow; they toil not, they spin not; . . . If God so clothe the grass, . . . how much more shall he clothe you, O ye of little faith? Seek ye first the kingdom of God; and all things shall be added unto you.—Luke.

Surely he shall deliver thee from the snare of the fowler and from the noisome pestilence.

Undoubtedly, Love shall release you from the entanglement of error and from destructive calamities.

If our earthly father responds to our call for help, surely our heavenly Father will supply our need. Religion devoid of healing is not what Christ taught and demanded of his followers. In the divine Word we read, "For I will restore health unto thee, and I will heal thee of thy wounds, saith the Lord."

Only as we know God's law and mentally declare and enforce it, in a very active way, do we realize the benefits of His goodness.

How can one become rightly acquainted with God? By gaining the spiritual understanding of the Bible and by working out the problems of life as Christ Jesus taught and practised.

A man can memorize the Bible from cover to cover; he can be entirely familiar with the lives and lessons of the prophets of the Old Testament; he can preach a glowing sermon about the words and works of the Saviour: and yet that same mortal may have no practical knowledge of God. A knowledge of God means something more than blind belief or a profession of faith. A knowledge of God to an individual means a spiritual consciousness of the all-presence and all-power of God. It means an operative, demonstrable knowledge which will save him from sickness and from sin.

Many people have an idea that they have accepted Christ when they have united with some church, accepted certain dogmas and creeds, and have been baptized after some form. We have found the Christ when we are able to love those who despitefully use us, when we judge not after the flesh. We have found the Christ, Truth, when we are able through spiritual understanding and uplifting to overcome mental and physical ills in ourselves and in others.

Salvation is not to be found in human resources nor in matter. Salvation is found in God alone.

Are we not losing valuable time and opportunity so long as we expect to be saved by anything else than Omnipotence?

Salvation is at our very door. It is indeed possible to be free now, free from trouble, from sin, from pain and discord. But we must not reject the very essentials of salvation. Redemption is within us. We must part with ignorance, indifference, self-righteousness, and the sins that would so easily beset us, and through the enlightened understanding we must put on charity, spiritual knowledge, and the fruits of love. Because of the changed condition of our thought Love delivers us from error.

Call upon me in the day of trouble: I will deliver thee, and thou shalt glorify me. The righteous cry, and the Lord heareth, and delivereth them out of all their troubles.—Psalms.

He shall cover thee with his feathers, and under his wings shalt thou trust: his truth shall be thy shield and buckler.

Divine Truth shall continually protect you, and upon His care shall you depend. The truth about God and man shall be your armor, your protection and defence.

With what tender love the Shepherd guards his sheep! How watchfully He cares for them! Infinite Love is ever-ready, ever-willing, to protect and deliver all who make His truth their shield and buckler. What is truth but right thinking demonstrated? The demonstrations of our knowledge of truth are to be seen in holiness, health, and happiness. In no other way can men arrive at these conditions of mind and body but through the truth, the understanding, of God and man.

If God is Infinite Spirit, Life, and Love, what is man? Man is the spiritual image and likeness of God. Man cannot be material, nor can he be created from dust, because the Bible states that

God created man in His own image. Some people mistakenly believe that, if man is like God, then God must be somewhat like a magnified man. But this idea of God is not the right one to hold. Man's likeness to God is in the mental and spiritual realm, not in matter or in flesh. God is everywhere as Life, Soul, Mind, Truth, Love, and man reflects the divine Consciousness.

Everything that is opposed to God or good, everything that differs from Love, the sole Creator, is not true or real, and is subject to annihilation. This is the truth which Christ Jesus said would make you free. We cannot eliminate evil by argument, but we can eliminate it by applying the truth. This truth shall be our shield and buckler, our protection and defence.

The true worshippers shall worship the Father in spirit and in truth. He that believeth on me, the works that I do shall he do also. If ye abide in me, and my words abide in you, ye shall ask what ye will, and it shall be done unto you. Herein is my Father glorified, that ye bear much fruit; so shall ye be my disciples.—John.

THE LIVING WAY

Thou shalt not be afraid for the terror by night; nor for the arrow that flieth by day; nor for the pestilence that walketh in darkness; nor for the destruction that wasteth at noonday.

You need not fear the voice of error or evil, for God is ever with you. In God's light there is no darkness.

Peace can only be obtained by following God in the right way. Life and Love are inseparable; so, also, are spiritual understanding and peace. A half-way trust is not what God requires. It is but a house built upon the sand or is like unto a man with two masters.

Do not give undue attention to the thoughts and opinions of others. Be not afraid of evil, be afraid only lest you do evil. If you belong to a long-established church, do not fear what your friends will say if you change your habits of thoughts. Know that God is more to you than all earthly interests. We should not allow the opinions of others to outweigh our convictions of right. Choose that religion which appeals most to your reason, irrespective of what your early religious training may have been. Discard all doctrines which do not follow the teachings of Christ Jesus. The religious beliefs of our fathers may be sacred to us because of tender associations and remembrances, but we should not hesitate to supplant them with a larger and grander thought of God.

The test of sincerity in religion hinges upon works, and not upon words. If we keep our minds well filled with thoughts of love and truth, there will be no room for thoughts of sin or of sickness.

Fear ye not the reproach of men, neither be ye afraid of their revilings. I, even I, am he that comforteth thee. No weapon that is formed against thee shall prosper; and every tongue that shall rise against thee in judgment thou shalt condemn. In righteousness shalt thou be established.—Isaiah.

A thousand shall fall at thy side and ten thousand at thy right hand; but it shall not come nigh thee. Only with thine eyes shalt thou behold and see the reward of the wicked.

The conditions called accidents, calamities, sickness, trouble, and sorrow, may come upon thousands around you, but they shall not harm you if you place your undivided confidence in God.

The medium through which we look has much to do with what is seen. The best already exists for every one of us, and always has existed. It remains for us to become spiritually-minded and see the good already in store for us. Were men to live in truth, love, and justice, there would be no evil in the universe.

To attribute any dual nature to God bars the door to heaven or harmony. God's knowledge is infinite, and is all-inclusive good. Neither to-day, any more than in the day of Elijah, is God to be found in the earthquake, in the fire, or in the whirlwind. Now, as always, God is found in the still, small voice of truth.

Sickness, sin, death, poverty, and suffering of every kind belong not to God's kingdom, and they are in the world because of the mortal belief in a power apart from God. No evil comes from God, and it is unknown to God.

According to the Scriptures, mortal existence is "of few days and is full of trouble." The consciousness of sin, disease, and death, is but a dream, and the knowledge of God awakens one from this dream. Sin, fear, and ignorance are the prolific sources of all human ills. Hell is mental and physical pain produced by wrong thinking. Heaven is the absence of fear, and is the consciousness of truth, righteousness, and love.

Whoso hearkeneth unto me shall dwell safely, and shall be quiet from fear of evil. In the way of righteousness is life; and in the pathway thereof there is no death.— Proverbs.

Because thou hast made the Lord, which is my refuge, even the Most High, thy habitation; there shall no evil befall thee; neither shall any plague come nigh thy dwelling.

Because you have made the Lord your first consideration, no error shall assail you, nor shall any discord come nigh your dwelling.

It is related of King Asa that, when he was diseased in his feet, he sought not to the Lord, but to physicians, and he died. This calls our attention to the fact that, should we look to means other than God in our hour of need, we disobey the law of God, and reap the consequences for so doing.

The condition of security is indicated in the words, "Because thou hast made the Lord thy habitation." In proportion as divine Truth becomes all-in-all to us will evil find no abiding-place in our consciousness. The demonstrations of health and harmony which follow an intelligent reliance upon God evidence the fact that we have found the pearl of great price, and that we have entered the path which leads to a present understanding of eternal life.

Religion is not to prepare men for death, the grave, and a future localized heaven. Learning the truth about God and man is the passport to a present heaven. The injunction, "Prepare to meet thy God," need not suggest a death scene. It need not strike terror into the hearts of men, nor should it be used as a slogan during revival seasons. People will never be driven into heaven through fear nor through death. We are in eternity now, and God will never be any nearer to us than He is now; for now "in him we live and have our being." The way to God is in the path of love.

Instead of thinking that we shall meet God after we die, we should know that we are meeting God now. He is our great Physician, our Father-Mother, our very life itself. If we find God now, we find heaven now.

All the beauty and grandeur of earth and heaven are at hand, and God is the living presence, pulsating the universe and man. Nothing but the veil of material sense hides from mortals the presence of heaven.

What doth it profit, my brethren, if a man say he hath faith, and have not works? can faith save him? Faith, if it hath not works, is dead. Be ye doers of the word, and not hearers only.—James.

For he shall give his angels charge over thee, to keep thee in all thy ways. They shalt bear thee up in their hands lest thou dash thy foot against a stone. Thou shalt tread upon the lion and adder: the young lion and the dragon shalt thou trample under feet.

Thoughts of love and truth protect and preserve you, guide your steps and deliver you from danger. Because of the spiritual condition of your thoughts, you shield yourself from error of every sort.

Angels are the spiritual intuitions and aspirations which pass between God and men. These pure thoughts and illuminations keep men from temptation, evil, and sin.

Our Master solved life's problems according to divine law. He acquainted men with their heavenly parent. He comforted the sorrowing, healed the sick, revealed the way to holiness, and taught the universal salvation of all men from evil, discord, sin, disease, and death. The day of miracles is not past. There is no reason why a believer in the teachings of Christ Jesus should doubt that his teachings are practical to-day. The way of salvation from evil has not changed.

What must I do to be saved? saved from every kind of error? Let in the light of God. Darkness is not something, but rather is it the lack of something,— the lack of light. The light of understanding brings healing to mind and body, and the human consciousness becomes obedient to the divine.

Evil seems very real indeed to the one who thinks it; but, as we turn from evil, we become more spiritual, and realize more clearly the reality of good and the unreality of evil.

Do not think you are doing all you can because you keep your erroneous thoughts to yourself. It is wise indeed to guard our speech, but, when the thought becomes guarded, there will be little necessity for guarding the speech.

In the vocabulary of Spirit there appears no such word as can't. Men are given all the time necessary, in which they can work out their salvation. Were this not true, God would not require it of them.

He that overcometh shall inherit all things; and I will be his God, and he shall be my son.

Now is come salvation, and strength, and the kingdom of our God, and the power of his Christ.—Revelation.

Because he has set his love upon me, therefore will I deliver him; I will set him on high, because he hath known my name.

In proportion as we place our love and trust in God are we delivered from discordant conditions.

How can one measure his love for God? and what makes men Christian? Our love for God can be measured by our love for man. Some people hang their hope of salvation on their Sunday hypocrisy. Attendance at church or belief about God and Christ does not make a Christian. A Christian is one who possesses the mind of Christ. A Christian is one who knows the way which Jesus taught and practised and who follows in his steps. Christ said, "I am the way," and plainly indicated that he considered himself an example for his followers.

Jesus recognized only the good in others: therefore, his love was "without dissimulation." Love is the greatest of all human attainments. All gifts of mind, however excellent, are worth nothing without love.

Let love be without dissimulation. Be ye of the same mind one toward another. Love worketh no ill to his neighbor; therefore, love is the fulfilling of the law.— Romans.

*He shall call upon me, and I will answer him: I will be with him in trouble;
I will deliver him, and honor him. With long life will I satisfy him, and show him my salvation.*

As humans, we all err, and we can rise above error only as we see and correct it and cease to sin. All the sins of the world will vanish under the every-day application of the truth. Every man has his Achilles' heel or some faulty condition of thought. Let us search out the vulnerable condition, and make haste to overcome our weaknesses. If we do not want discordant conditions in the body, we must abide in love.

It is only by constant growth, the continual rising from the things that we put under our feet, that we can ever attain our spiritual birthright,—perfection. This growth in thought and character comes through loving, earnest, persistent, watchful activity; by striving for the perfect realization of the ideal which has been set for us in the life and teachings of Christ Jesus.

The teaching that God is good, but man is a sinner, has separated men from intelligence and has deprived them of spiritual power and strength.

God never made a sick, sinning mortal, but He made a free, spiritual man. God is positive and active. Human ignorance makes evil seem resistant, but evil is attractive only to those who are ignorant of good. Sin and sickness were brought about by a false conception of life, and it is through spiritual illumination and prayer that they can be destroyed. He who heals through prayer has the Bible for his authority and Christ Jesus for his example.

Suppose all the world believed that there are no laws of health except the law of righteousness; no medicine except the truth that man is the image of God, made spiritual, free, and perfect; no surgery except the excision of all erroneous thoughts, habits, and beliefs; no mind except the mind of Christ, the mind of love, honesty, good-will toward men: would not this be heaven, and would not the highest purpose of religion be realized?

I will give unto him that is athirst of the fountain of life freely. Behold, I stand at the door, and knock: if any man hear my voice, and open the door, I will come in to him, and will sup with him, and he with me.—Revelation.

APR 26 1912

Lightning Source UK Ltd.
Milton Keynes UK
UKHW020652250123
415939UK00007B/392